Loretta Santini

Verona

Art and History

Published and printed by

NARNI - TERNI

index

PHOTOGRAPHS: archivio Plurigraf - Bagnasco - Barone - Bianchi - Ganzaroli - Pubbliaerfoto
AERIAL PHOTOS AUTORIZATION: concess. S.M.A. 0003 del 5-1-76
Map by kind permission of Azienda Promozione Turistica di Verona

Verona, the city of Romeo and Juliet

Verona is a splendid city; monumental, elegant and romantic. The River Adige runs through it at a leisurely pace, creating two great loops which reflect the city's magnificent monuments and seem to embrace and jealously guard its extraordinary historical, cultural and artistic heritage.

Defined as the "gateway of Italy" in view of its geographical position on the foothills of the Alps and at the mouth of the Adige valley, the city is known throughout the world as the setting for the star-crossed love affair of Romeo and Juliet, the two characters in Shakespeare's tragedy of the same name.

Its fame is also linked to the majestic Arena where every year important cultural events take place, the most prestigious being the opera season, which finds, in the Roman Amphitheatre, an outstanding natural backdrop and a setting which proves particularly suitable for the performance of works with large sets.

However, Verona is above all a beautiful city: its monuments, its squares - especially Piazza delle Erbe, Piazza dei Signori and Piazza Bra' - its churches (San Zeno Maggiore, the Cathedral, Sant'Anastasia and San Fermo Maggiore), bear outstanding witness to its history and art down the centuries.

The Roman city, the mediaeval city and the city of the della Scala family - that is to say the periods which marked the main stages of its urban development - are perfectly blended together: they exist side by side in complete harmony and together create an historic centre of enor-

Romantic reconstruction of the lovers' meeting between Romeo and Juliet.

mous distinction. Verona played a leading role in events of the utmost importance: it was the birthplace or workplace of personalities of great stature: Catullus, the refined Latin poet; Vitruvius, author of the most famous treatise on art in ancient times; Saint Zeno the black bishop who became the city's patron saint; the Ostrogoth Theodoric; Alboin, king of the Lombards, who met his death in Verona at the hand of his wife Rosmunda; Pepin, son of Charlemagne and finally the Scaligeri - rulers and benefac-

tors of the city - the most famous of whom was Cangrande Della Scala.

Today's Verona is both vibrant and elegant: its ancient monumental centre, which has remained virtually intact, constitutes the hub of its past history and is a favourite destination for tourists from all over the world, who flock to see its sights.

The modern city - which has expanded beyond the historic centre and since the end of the Second World War has greatly enlarged its urban fabric - has developed a complex of economic activities (agriculture, industry, trade) which make it one of the busiest centres in Italy. A prime example of this is the Verona Fair, one of the most highly-rated venues for the development of the agroindustrial sector. In addition, the city still today maintains its role as the "gateway of Europe" and is a favoured place for product marketing.

Yet what lodges most in the heart of anyone visiting Verona is the atmosphere which imbues the town houses, the churches and the beautiful, striking squares.

The memory and the image of the balcony onto which Juliet stepped out to talk to her beloved Romeo, the tomb on which their bittersweet affair was finally burnt out, the tormenting reminder of a beautiful yet tragic love story will linger on above all. A story and a tradition which have given Verona the title of **"city of love"**.

Della Scala Tombs - detail of the tomb of Cansignorio. Of the funeral monuments erected for the Della Scala family, the tomb of Cansignorio, executed in 1375 by Bonino da Campione and Gaspare Broaspini, is the most magnificent and is surmounted, above the canopy, by the equestrian statue of the ruler of Verona.

Artistic and historical outline

The origins of Verona are very ancient: prehistoric settlements have been found in the area of San Pietro along the course of the River Adige - a naturally defended place and facilitated in its communications by the proximity of the waterway - and in the neighbouring territory in the area corresponding to the Via Postumia. Mention is made of an inhabited centre at the beginning of the 4th century B.C. By the 2nd century B.C. the inhabited centre had spread along the right bank of the river. Later evidence regarding the city's urban development dates back to the Roman occupation of 49 B.C. An inscription found on the Porta dei Leoni records the names of the *"quattuorviri"* (magistrates) who set in motion the works to organize the city centre. Having become a colony in 89 B.C., Verona became a nodal point along the consular roads which crossed the north of Italy: these were the Via Augusta, the Via Gallica and the Via Postumia (opened in 148 B.C. by Spurius Postumius Albinus) which, following older routes, formed a link with the Po plain, with Milan and with Genoa respectively. Verona extended its inhabited centre into the territory within the loop of the River Adige and very soon acquired the urban structure typical of Roman cities: a grid-based plan realized by the intersection of the cardinal and decuman roads and the streets running parallel to them. It was also provided with an effective system of fortifications and gates and enriched with magnificent monuments. These are the same monuments whose ruins make present-day Verona one of the richest cities in Italy as regards vestiges of the past. It is sufficient to cite the example of the splendid and famous Arena of Verona, the ancient Amphitheatre of the Imperial age. Also worthy of mention are the Theatre, the gates (Porta dei Leoni), the bridges (Ponte Lapideo or Ponte Pietra and Ponte Postumio), the arches (the Gavi Arch). In the imperial epoch, thanks to the importance which it had attained, it was given the honorary title of *"Colonia Augusta"*. Among the illustrious sons of this city were the Latin poet Catullus and Vitruvius, author of a systematic treatise on art. First in the late empire and then in the Middle Ages the city was the venue for major events: its strategic position and its role as a gateway to the Po plain made it the scene of battles between Claudius and the Germans (268 A.D.) and between Constantine and Maxentius (402 A.D.) and it was a focal point of passage and dominion of various peoples; these were the Ostrogoths under Theodoric (493-526), the Lombards under Alboin (569-573), and the Carolingians, who from Charlemagne to Berengar, that is until 924, made the city a centre of art and culture as well as the capital of the Kingdom. After the invasion of the Hungarians and the period marked by feudal struggles Verona became a free Commune.

It was the 12th century. The city witnessed huge commercial development and, consequently, a decisive increase in the population and impressive urban growth. Verona had more than once extended the vast complex of defensive walls and had strengthened the bridges and the points of greatest strategic importance. Now more churches were built (the Cathedral, the basilica of San Zeno, San Fermo, San

Lorenzo, San Giovanni in Valle and SS. Trinità), as well as town houses and monasteries (San Zeno, San Fermo and Santa Maria in Organo). After 1261 and the feudal interlude of Ezzelino Romano, famous for his cruelty and despotism, the rule of the Scaligeri began, which was to leave an indelible mark on the city.

The greatest and best-known member of this family was Cangrande della Scala (1291-1329). Verona witnessed a golden age: it strengthened its defences (a new boundary wall was built), the urban space was reorganized and enlarged, in particular Piazza delle Erbe and Piazza dei Signori with the construction of the hous-

es which still surround them today. In addition, the city was embellished with new monuments including prestigious mansions, castles - Castelvecchio was built at the behest of Cansignorio -, churches, houses (including that of the Montecchi family), as well as with the so-called della Scala Tombs, the funeral monuments of the rulers of Verona. Fourteenth century painting reached its maximum expression in the works of Turone and Altichiero.

In 1387 it came under the Visconti; in 1405 it became part of the Venetian Republic under which it remained, with changing fortunes and short periods of interruption, until the French Revolution (1796). In the artistic field the personalities of greatest importance were first and foremost Stefano da Verona and Pisanello, then Andrea Mantegna and, in the architectural field, Sammicheli in particular, who was to leave most of his masterpieces in the city. From the town-planning point of view Verona witnessed a gradual militarization of its defensive systems (construction of walls and the fortress-buildings of Castel San Felice and Castel San Pietro) and a similarly gradual reorganization of the spaces which were to answer, in a functional way, the new economic and administrative needs of the city, which required more services and more infrastructure. At the end of the 18th century it came under the Lombard-Veneto Kingdom dependent on Austria, but part of the city, the part on the left bank commonly known as "Veronetta", however, remained under France. It was part of the so-called "quadrilateral" (the Hapsburgs had strengthened the city defences through the construction of advanced forts in the defensive wall, the so-called "roundels"), the group of cities - the others were Peschiera, Legnago and Mantova - which represented the military strongholds of the kingdom, with whose fate it was inextricably linked until 1866, the year in which, as a consequence of the 3rd war of independence, it became part of the Kingdom of Italy.

The story of Romeo and Juliet

Romeo Montecchi and Juliet Capuleti, having met at a masked ball, fall hopelessly in love with one another. Owing to the great rivalry between the two families the two young people are forced to meet under cover. Their secret but happy marriage is devastated by tragic events: Romeo, having avenged his friend Mercutio, murdered by Tybalt, cousin of Juliet, is forced to flee from Verona. The young girl in the meantime, so as not to marry the man who is being forced on her by her father, on the advice of Friar Laurence, drinks a potion which makes her appear to be dead. The message which she sends to Romeo to explain to her beloved the stratagem behind her apparent death, unfortunately arrives too late. Romeo, having returned to Verona, on beholding his lifeless bride takes his life and Juliet, having awoken from her long sleep, on seeing what has taken place, stabs herself through the heart and dies in the arms of her husband. The families of the two young lovers, faced with their great love and the appalling tragedy, become reconciled.

The tragic story recounted by Shakespeare has been found to have any historical foundation.

There certainly existed a tale

which spoke of a thwarted love affair and which finished tragically. Previously, Dante, having lived in exile in Verona between 1299 and 1304, in the Divine Comedy (Purgatory, canto VI, 106-108) had made reference to the rivalry between the two families: "Come to see Montecchi and Cappelletti,...". The critics, however, maintain that the two names stand for two parties (imperial and anti imperial) who were in conflict throughout the area of Lombardy and Veneto. The presence in Verona of monuments (Romeo's house, Juliet's house, Juliet's tomb) related to the story, provides a glimpse of a factual foundation for the story without, however, providing any certainty.

In addition, there is evidence of the existence of a family named Dal Cappello which might recall that of the Capuleti.

Even if we cannot set the seal on the truth of the love affair and rivalry between the two families, it is gratifying to think that the story of Romeo and Juliet did actually take place and that, despite its unhappy ending, it continues to be the symbol of the intense passion which can exist between young people.

Verona, the *city of love* (a sort of twinning has been established with Terni, birthplace of Saint Valentine, the patron saint of lovers) has organized a series of cultural events which seek to remember and reinforce the story of Romeo and Juliet. The most original and charming of the many is that which has organized the collection of love messages. These are letters, poems, confessions and testimonials addressed to "Romeo and Juliet, Verona" which arrive in their thousands from all over the world.

Places connected with Romeo and Juliet

Romeo's house

This is the name given to what tradition has it is the house of the Montecchi family and of Romeo, the Shakespearean character who had a tragic love affair with Juliet. It is actually the house of Cagnolo Nogarola and is a fourteenth century building in the Gothic style organized around various inner courtyards. The walls are covered in brick and the upper part has a crenellated coping.

Juliet's house

This building (13th century), not far from the Piazza delle Erbe, is the one indicated by tradition as being the house of the Capuleti family and hence of the unfortunate Juliet. The brick construction is enhanced by beautiful trilobed windows and, above all, by the elegant and famous **balcony** onto which, according to tradition, the young girl stepped out to talk to Romeo. In the courtyard is a statue depicting the young girl by N. Costantini. The typical features of a fourteenth century

house have been reconstructed inside and an interesting collection of ceramics is on display. The delightful, though sad, story related by the great English dramatist has made of this place and of this balcony, the symbol of love affairs and has even turned it into a place of pilgrimage.

Juliet's tomb

Tradition has it that the tomb in the former **Convent of the Franciscans** is that of Juliet. The evocative setting contributes to the visitor's immersion in the sad and sorrowful atmosphere of the Shakespearean tale: the tomb is a marble sarcophagus of the 13th-14th century supported by stone slabs.

The historic centre: Piazza delle Erbe and Piazza dei Signori

The complex of these two squares constitutes the monumental centre of Verona, the ideal centre of the political and administrative life of the past, from the Verona of the Roman epoch to that of the Della Scala period. Both squares are splendid as far as the monuments which stand on them are concerned and in terms of their characteristic atmosphere, yet in appearance they are quite distinct: the former intimate, evocative and lively, the latter refined and elegant, they both express important stages in the city's historical and artistic development.

Piazza delle Erbe

Picturesque and lively with its multitude of market stalls covered by characteristic umbrellas - hence its name - it is also one

Catullus

Gaius Valerius Catullus was born in Verona in '87 B.C., lived for a long time in Rome and died in Sirmione in 54 B.C. He was one of the greatest Latin poets. He wrote the Carmina, poetic compositions mostly consisting of epigrams and elegies, in which he deals, in a refined and elegant way, with the subjects of friendship and love for Lesbia.

Cangrande Della Scala

The Scaligeri, (or Della Scala), a noble Venetian family, started their rule of Verona in 1263 under Mastino I, but reached their moment of greatest power under Cangrande I (1291-1329), an enlightened ruler and patron of writers and artists. He was the imperial vicar of Enrico VII. Under him the borders of the Della Scala territory were extended as far as Belluno, Padua and Treviso. The exiled Dante Alighieri was a guest at his court from 1303 to 1316, after the earlier opportunity afforded him to appreciate the city under Bartolomeo I.
The Seigniory of the Della Scala declined in 1387 and was replaced by that of Gian Galeazzo Visconti.

San Zeno

Of African origin - he was known as "the Moor" - he lived in the 4th century and was Bishop of Verona.
He was the author of Homilies and proudly fought against paganism by converting the local population to Christianity. His feast day is celebrated on 12th April.

of the best known and best loved squares of poets and writers from all over the world, so much so that it has come to be considered "the most beautiful monument" in the city. It is surrounded by buildings whose architecture is often unusual and irregular in terms of height. Some bear traces of frescoes which accentuate the colourful atmosphere of the square.

The area on which the square stands is the same as that occupied by the Forum, the ancient centre of the political, administrative and economic life of the Roman city. It was originally much larger (57 metres in width and 168 metres in length), but after it became the economic, political and administrative centre of Communal Verona it was scaled down to its present-day dimensions by the construction of important public buildings.

The name of the Piazza delle Erbe comes from the role played by this area in the Della Scala era, when it functioned as the town's economic centre.

Piazza delle Erbe - Fountain of Madonna Verona. The statue is so-called because it is considered to be the symbol of the city. The scroll which she holds in her hands bears the municipal motto: "Est iusti latrix urbs haec et laudus amatrix".

The buildings in the Piazza delle Erbe

In the central area of the square stand the Market column, the pillory, the fountain of Madonna Verona and the column of San Marco.

The **Market column** dates back to 1401: it was designed to support the insignia of the nobles. The **Pillory** is a sixteenth century work. It was the place used for ceremonies and public investitures and consists of a marble aedicule resting on four pillars.

The **Fountain of Madonna Verona** is a water-basin executed in 1368 by Giovanni Rigino using in part a thermal basin: at the centre stands a statue of the Roman age found among the ruins of the ancient *Capitolium* and representing a girl. This statue, christened *"Madonna Verona"*, is considered as the symbol of the city and was placed on the fountain at the behest of Cansignorio, who thereby intended to commemorate the restoration and the re-opening of the city aqueduct. In her hands she holds the communal motto *"Est iusti latrix urbs haec et laudus amatrix"*.

The **Column of San Marco** was erected in 1523 by Michele Leoni and was designed to support the *lion of Saint Mark* (the present-day statue is a nineteenth century copy). It symbolized the subjection of Verona to Venice.

South-west side of the square:

Past the solid frontage of the **tower-houses** of the ancient Ghetto, stands the **Domus Mercatorum**, with a fine arcade and double lancet windows, built at the behest of Alberto I della Scala in 1301. The building, once intended as a headquarters for the guilds, had part of its primitive Romanesque-Gothic structure altered owing to nineteenth century modifications.

There then follow several Renaissance buildings such as the **Cristani House** (on the facade *frescoes* of a sacred subject by Girolamo dai Libri).

The far side of the square is closed off by the **Torre del**

Piazza delle Erbe - the baroque facade of Palazzo Maffei.

Right-hand photo: the Municipal Tower.
Left-hand photo: Overall view of the Piazza delle Erbe, the city's lively centre, crowded with market stalls.

The term "marangona" would seem to derive from "maragon" which, in the local dialect, means "carpenter". It is supposed, therefore, that the bell, as it struck the hours, would announce the beginning and the end of the working day. "Rengo" on the other hand refers to the term "arringo" or "arengo" (square or area used for tournaments or meetings of the city Council) and was probably intended to assemble the people. This bell is the larger of the two and was cast in 1557 by Alessandro Bonaventurini.

Gardello or Torre delle Ore (a tower built at the behest of Cansignorio in the second half of the 14th century) and **Palazzo Maffei** in Baroque style (conversion of a building originating from the 13th century), with a richly decorated facade and completed with a balustrade surmounted by *statues* depicting ancient divinities. Initially it belonged to the Dal Verme family and then passed to the famous condottiere Erasmo da Narni known as the Gattamelata.
North-east side of the square: What remains of the **Domus Bladorum** (complex of warehouses and shops) is still visible, converted in the 16th century into the **Mazzanti Houses**. There is an interesting facade consisting of alternate marble and frescoed squares (*allegorical scenes*) by the artist Alberto Cavalli, a pupil of Giulio Romano (16th century). The rear part of the building is also very fine and has preserved part of the mediaeval structure and an interesting courtyard.
Domus nova: this building, the ancient headquarters of the

Podestà, was extensively reorganized in the mid-17th century and in the 18th century was raised.
Palazzo del Comune: built in the 12th century, it reveals, on the side which juts out over Piazza delle Erbe, a neoclassical superstructure. The facade which looks out over Piazza dei Signori was also reorganized in part during the Renaissance era. This building contains a noteworthy courtyard - the **Old Market** - embellished with three-mullioned windows and a marble staircase. It is flanked by two towers, one of which is the **Torre dei Lamberti** which is 84 metres tall and soars above the other city towers. Its construction (in tuff and marble), initiated in the 12th century, was finished in the 15th century with the addition of the belfry. The latter contains the historic bells of Verona: the **Rengo** and the **Marangona**.
Arco della Costa: the Arch of the Rib takes its name from the whale "rib" hanging from it and is perhaps a replica of a pre-existent arch.

Piazza dei Signori

This area is linked to the adjoining Piazza delle Erbe by the Arco della Costa. Defined as the "drawing room of Verona", its monumental and elegant appearance was conferred on it by the Della Scala Seigniory. Of noteworthy interest are the buildings which border it, mostly characterized by slender and airy arcades. At its centre stands the **monument to Dante Alighieri** who, during his exile, was the guest of the Della Scala family from 1303 to 1316. It is the work of Ugo Zannoni (1865). The **Palazzo del Comune** (or Palazzo della Ragione), built in the 12th century, shows on this side (the other faces Piazza delle Erbe) the facade renovated in the Renaissance era. The inner courtyard, known as the **Old Market**, contains the very fine **Della Ragione staircase**). Past a fourteenth century crenellated tower stands the imposing building of the **Palazzo del Capitanio** - so called because, under Venice, it was the seat of the Captain of Verona - which was the result of the amalgamation of a se-

ries of tower-houses, the facade being redesigned in the 16th century. There is a fine *portal*, the work of Sammicheli and a magnificent ***courtyard*** distinguished by the elegant **Loggia Barbaro** and the **Porta Bombardiera** (1687), so called owing to its highly original decoration which consists of copies of weapons and symbols of war. At the far end of the square stands the **Palazzo degli Scaligeri** or **Palazzo della Prefettura**, formerly **Palazzo del Governo**, whose construction, which began in the 12th century, continued until the end of the 14th century and later underwent various modifications. There is a fine ***Courtyard*** and a double ***loggia*** with Gothic and round arches which dates back to the original building. The spectacular **Loggia del Consiglio** (also known as the **Loggia di fra' Giocondo**, from the name of its probable designer), the ancient seat of the city Council, was built at the end of the 15th century in beautiful Renaissance style. The lower part is embellished by an airy arcade; a fine series of double lancet windows opens out of the

upper fascia, closed in between refined pilasters and surmounted by arched gables. On the top stand various *statues* depicting illustrious personages of the past by Alberto da Milano: Catullus, Pliny, Marcus, Vitruvius and Cornelius Nepos. The amber colour of the walls further enhances the beauty and atmosphere of the building. The square is closed off by the **Domus Nova**, a building bordering on the adjacent Piazza delle Erbe. Its present-day aspect is that conferred on it at the end of the 17th century. The raised part on the other hand dates back to the first half of the 18th century. The so-called **Volto della Tortura** leads into the Piazzaletto delle Arche.

Photo above: the Lamberti Tower.
Photo below: overall view of the Piazza dei Signori with the monument to Dante, the Loggia del Consiglio and, in the background, the Palazzo del Capitanio with its fine sixteenth century portal by Sammicheli.
Opposite page: detail of the elegant Della Ragione Staircase.

Piazzaletto delle Arche

This small and highly distinctive space admirably completes the complex of squares in the historic centre and provides a splendid example of building in the della Scala epoch. It was in fact on this site, next to their residence, that the Rulers of Verona commissioned the construction of the family Cemetery - the della Scala Tombs - and the church of Santa Maria Antica.

The Della Scala Tombs

These are the funeral monuments of the della Scala family. A marble surround on which rests a wrought iron railing encloses an area where the tombs (sarcophagi) and the statues of the rulers of Verona are preserved. In particular, the visitor can admire the **Tomb of Cangrande I**, that of **Mastino II**, that of **Cansignorio** and the **sarcophagus of Alberto I**. The other tombs belong to Mastino I, Bartolomeo, Alboin and Cangrande II.

Tomb of Cangrande I

This is the sepulchral monument of Cangrande I della Scala (1291-1329) and stands by the Church of Santa Maria Antica. The monument is in the Romanesque style and is the work of the Master of Sant'Anastasia. The tomb, surrounded by a stone enclosure, consists of a canopy leaning on columns and surmounted by a cusp. Above is the statue of Cangrande (copy of the original housed in the Castelvecchio Museum). The sides of the sarcophagus are sculpted in bas-relief.

Tomb of Mastino II

A railing adorned with statues encloses the tomb, whose lid de-

Photo above: Piazza dei Signori - Monument to Dante Alighieri, the poet who was the guest of the Della Scala family.
Opposite page: the Loggia dei Signori, also known as the Loggia di fra' Giocondo, a Renaissance construction (15th century) which was the ancient seat of the city Council.

picts the figure of Mastino II while the faces of the sepulchre are sculpted with decorations and bas-reliefs. The whole is covered by a richly decorated canopy culminating in the *equestrian statue* of the same Mastino.

Tomb of Cansignorio

Is certainly the most striking of the Della Scala tombs. It was built for Cansignorio, who died in 1375, by Bonino da Campione and Gaspare Broaspini. The tomb is placed inside a railing where, within various richly decorated niches surmounted by spires are the statues of various *Saints*. A sumptuous canopy resting on spiral columns and embellished with niches, aedicules, pinnacles and statues, hangs over the sepulchre, which is

also adorned with a wealth of decoration: the bas-reliefs depict *Episodes linked to the life of Cansignorio.*

Romeo's House Juliet's House

The two houses are not far from one another: they are indicated by tradition as being the residences of the Capuleti and Montecchi families, a fact which is anything but certain.

On the front of the so-called House of Juliet, the visitor can admire the delightful **balcony** - famous throughout the world - which she stepped out onto so that she might talk to her beloved. In the courtyard is the statue by the sculptor Nereo Costantini.

Church of Santa Maria Antica

A fine example of Veronese Romanesque architecture, it was built in the 7th century A.D., but was substantially modified at the end of the 12th century. The alternation of fascias of stone and brick create, above all in the interior, an intimate and striking atmosphere.

Municipal Library

Founded at the end of the 18th century it contains one of the most important and richest Italian collections of incunabula, codices and manuscripts (some very rare), of enormous documentary value. There is also a splendid collection of ancient prints.

Church of Sant'Anastasia with its beautiful double portal.

Porta dei Leoni

Also known as Porta Leona it is one of the old Roman gates. It was built in the 1st century B.C. (but was subsequently modified) along the circuit of the defensive walls and at the exit of the major cardinal road axis.

Today it is partly mutilated - the lower part is the most visible - and is partly hidden by the town house which has been built next to it.

What remains of it still reveals its harmonious and balanced architecture: its design inspired many artists in the Renaissance period.

Careful research in recent years has brought to light other elements of the Roman age in the shape of sections of paving and the bases of defence towers of the walls themselves.

Via Sottoriva

This is perhaps the most characteristic street in the old mediaeval centre of Verona. The street is wedged between ancient houses such as the **Houses of the Monselice** of the 13th and 14th century (particularly worthy of admiration are the beautiful single and double lancet windows) and it is, for the most part, arcaded.

Church of Santa Maria della Scala

The construction of the building, sponsored by Cangrande I della Scala, dates back to the first half of the 14th century, but underwent remarkable modifications in the 16th century and after the last world war. It contains works by Giolfino and the *Stories of St. Jerome and other Saints*, the work of Giovanni

Badile (15th century), one of the most important works of international Gothic.

Church of Sant'Anastasia

The church belonged to the Dominicans and was built on the site of a smaller older church dedicated to the same Saint at the end of the 13th century and finished - with the exception of the facade whose entire upper part is uncovered - in 1481. The front shows the division into three naves and a very fine ***portal*** with a double opening framed within a composite series of elegant pointed arches. It is decorated with polychrome marbles and bas-reliefs of a sacred subject depicting the *Stories of the New Testament, Stories of Saint Anastasia and St. Peter the Martyr* and *Stories of the Dominicans*. The interior, solemn, majestic and soaring, shows a blend of Romanesque and Gothic styles: the three naves are separated by large columns supporting refined Gothic capitals and pointed arches. The frescoed vaults with floral motifs, which have been restored to a large extent by numerous repaintings, are a breathtaking sight. The central nave ends in the transept and in the splendid, luminous apse with high single lancet windows opening out of it. The marble **pavement** was executed in the 15th century by Pietro da Porlezza.

The church is embellished by a magnificent collection of paintings and sculptures.

In the central nave, alongside the first two columns the visitor can admire the **Hunchback holy water stoups**, so called because they are supported by two unusual curved figures. The one on the left is attributed to G. Caliari, father of the painter Paolo Veronese. Among the most important works in the right nave, worthy of note are the **altar of the Fregoso family**, a 16th century work by Cattaneo and Sammicheli, the *altar of San Vincenzo Ferreri* by Pietro Porlezza (2nd chapel) and various frescoes, including a *Deposition* by Liberale da Verona.

In the Centrengo Chapel - last on the right - the *altar of Saint Thomas Aquinas* is decorated with the splendid altar-piece by Girolamo dai Libri depicting the **Madonna and Child with Saints**.

The Transept gives on to five chapels.

Cavalli Chapel: it contains the large votive fresco by Altichiero depicting **The Cavalli family presented to the Virgin**, a work of the second half of the 14th century (right-hand wall, top); a *Madonna enthroned* (14th century); the statue of *San Geminiano* by the Master of Sant'Anastasia (in the niche) and the *tombs of the Cavalli family.*

Pellegrini Chapel: the famous fresco by Pisanello of *Saint George freeing the Princess*, a masterpiece of flamboyant Gothic, which is now found above the entry arch to the Chapel. The Chapel contains, in addition to fifteenth century *frescoes* and the *tombs* of the Pellegrini family, an interesting series of **24 terracotta tiles** depicting *Episodes from the life of Jesus* executed by Michele da Firenze in 1435.

Presbytery or **Great Chapel**: its soaring Gothic lines lend it great elegance and harmony.

Church of Sant'Anastasia - interior and detail of one of the so-called "hunchbacks", original curved figures which support the holy water stoups.

The right-hand wall is dominated by the great fresco of the **Last Judgement** attributed by some to Turone, by others to an artist identified only as the Master of the Last Judgement. There is a monumental **Sepulchre of Cortesia Serego**, attributed to Nicolò Lamberti. At the side of the monument is the fresco of the *Annunciation* (Michele Giambono) characterised by the flamboyant Gothic style.

Lavagnoli Chapel: in addition to the statue of the *Madonna and Saint Ann* the room is decorated with *frescoes* of the school of Mantegna.

Salerni Chapel: it contains the tombs of the Salerni family and various fifteenth century paintings. The transept gives onto the **Giusti Chapel** where the famous fresco by Pisanello of **Saint George freeing the Princess** has been placed, one of the masterpieces of Gothic art (international Gothic), an admirable work in terms of its balanced and skilful composition of the scene, and the elegance and refinement of the compositive lines. The figure in profile of the Princess of Silene is very beautiful and the landscape which unwinds in the background almost fairytale-like.

Church of Sant'Anastasia - view of the Romanesque-Gothic style interior. It is enhanced by chapels and embellished with numerous works of art by Pietro da Porlezza, (floor and altar of San Vincenzo Ferreri), Sammicheli, Liberale da Verona, Girolamo dai Libri and Pisanello.

Left-hand photo: detail of the holy water stoup with the statue of the "hunchback"

Opposite page: overall view of the interior with its frescoed vault.

SANTVS

Hunchback holy water stoups.
Church of Sant'Anastasia -
view of the interior.

Among the works which adorn the left-hand nave, worthy of mention is the *Madonna of the Rosary* (located in the 16th century monumental **Chapel of the Rosary**), greatly venerated by the Veronese in that she is considered to be their protectress. Works by G. B. Lorenzetti decorate the vault.

Next are an admirable *Organ*, a *Choir* of the 17th century and the *Miniscalchi altar*, a splendid Renaissance work by Giolfino. The 1st altar in polychrome marble is also a monumental sixteenth century work showing a wealth of sculptures, paintings and architectural features. The frescoes are by Francesco Morone.

Near the church of Sant'Anastasia is the **Tomb of Guglielmo di Castelbarco** sculpted by the Master of Sant'Anastasia, along with other tombs, all of which were, for the most part, executed between the 14th and the 15th century.

The small **Church of San Giorgetto dei Domenicani** is of interest, built at the end of the 13th century and today a venue for exhibitions. It contains fourteenth century frescos.

Photo on previous page: St. George freeing the Princess - Pisanello
It is one of the finest works in the international Gothic style: imbued with a fairytale-like, poetic atmosphere, it is characterized by its refined composition and the close attention paid to the costumes and naturalistic details.

Opposite page: panoramic view of the city - in the foreground the church of Sant'Anastasia.

Ponte Pietra

This bridge, also known as the Ponte Lapideo, was built in the Republican age - originally it was called "*marmoreus*" (made of marble) - together with the Ponte Postumius: the stone ashlars from that epoch which provided its framework are still visible, concentrated above all in the two colonnades on the left bank of the Adige.

The other three were reconstructed in the 16th century probably by Antonio Scarpagnino. The watch tower, on the other hand, belongs to the 13th century and was commissioned by Alberto I Della Scala.

The Ponte Pietra or Ponte Lapideo is the ancient "marmoreus" bridge, a Roman work of the Republican age. Only part of the original structure has survived; the rest belongs to the 16th century reconstruction.

Church of San Giovanni in Fonte

This small church was originally the baptistery of the Cathedral. The construction which we see today dates back to 1123, but its origins are even older.

The building is of simple design but various pictorial and sculptoral finds belonging to the primitive building are striking in their effect. The most important piece is the thirteenth century **baptismal font**, attributed to the sculptor Brialdo, who was active between 1189 and 1220, it is a monolithic basin with an octagonal plan. The external faces are entirely sculpted with bas-reliefs. The panels, separated by spiral pilasters and bordered on the upper part by a decoration of small hanging arches, depict: 1) *The Annunciation of the Virgin*, 2) *The Visitation to the Virgin*, 3) *The Nativity of Christ*, 4) *Christ's birth is announced to the shepherds*, 5) *The Epiphany*, 6) *Herod*, 7) *The Slaughter of the Innocents*, 8) *The Baptism of Christ*.

Church of San Giovanni in Fonte - it was the old Cathedral baptistery - the baptismal font is a monolithic octagonal-shaped basin whose sides are sculpted in bas-relief.

Church of Sant'Elena

This small yet delightful church was built in the 12th century on the ruins of an Early Christian building of the 9th century of which some remains have been brought to light. The interior houses a magnificent ***crucifix*** dating back to the 12th century, a painting by Brusasorci and a fourteenth century stone triptych. It is said that it was in this church that Dante Alighieri gave his opening address "De aqua et de terra" ("the question of water and of earth"). Recent studies have identified, in connection with the church of Sant'Elena, the remains of an ancient Early Christian building which can be traced back to the **Church of Santa Maria Matricolare**.

Cathedral District

The district around the Cathedral shows another side of Verona: less monumental, less well-known, but equally fascinating. This too is part of the ancient heart of the city: the streets wind silently between old buildings and small squares in solitary seclusion; the architecture of the houses and mansions, even those belonging to the aristocracy, is simple and contained. The pervading atmosphere here conjures up glimpses of the past and is intensely evocative of the way of life of bygone days.

Bishop's Palace

The architecture of this building is in the sixteenth century style although its origins must date back to the 1300s. The entrance door is adorned with statues of the *Madonna, St. Peter, St. Paul*

and *St. Michael* (the work of fra' Giovanni da Verona). It has an interesting courtyard characterized by the presence of the architectural structures of the apsidal part of the church of San Giovanni in Fonte and the Bishop's Tower. The columns are surmounted by beautiful sculpted capitals. The palace contains frescoes by Brusasorci.

Cathedral

The Cathedral stands on a small picturesque square.
Built on the site of an older religious edifice, it owes part of its architectural design to the 12th century: the structure was, however, modified, in the 15th and

16th centuries particularly. The design of the composite facade reveals the blend of the Romanesque and Gothic styles: in the central part is a characteristic and very fine double ***Porch*** designed by Master Nicolò, the architect responsible for the 12th century design of the church. The lower part - framing the main door - rests on spiral columels; the arch is decorated with friezes of bas-reliefs. The upper part has low supporting columns and a coping of small hanging arches.

In the photos: interior and exterior of the Cathedral.

The great **portal** is a magnificent work by the same Nicolò: in the lunette a bas-relief depicts the *Madonna and Child*. Worthy of note is the architecture on the right-hand side and that of the apse, examples of the refined art of the Veronese Romanesque style. A beautiful frieze accentuates the entire structure and the *portal* with a porch which opens out of the right-hand side. The bell-tower dates back, in the lower part to the 13th century, in the middle part to the 16th century, and in the upper part to the 20th century (architect - Fagiuoli). The interior, harmoniously structured and of great effect, is in the Romanesque-Gothic style. It is divided into three naves by large soaring pillars of the red marble of Verona supporting pointed arches with cross vaults above. Several chapels lead off the sides of the naves. The artistic works of art housed in the church are of considerable interest. Worthy of mention in the right-hand nave, in addition to the works by Liberale da Verona (*Adoration of the Magi*, a work much-admired by Vasari), Giolfino and Francesco Morone (remains of an altarpiece), are the chapel of the Sacrament and the Mazzanti chapel which houses the superb **Tomb of Saint Agatha** (14th century). The Presbytery is characterized by an elegant ***tornacoro***, a semicircle of Ionic columns designed by Sammicheli. The apse contains frescoes by Torbido depicting the *Annunciation, Episodes in the Life of Mary* and the *Prophets* (16th century). The left-hand nave, in addition to the works by Giovanni Caroto (*Madonna between Saints Martin and Stephen*), by Brusasorci and

Zannoni, houses the splendid masterpiece by Titian depicting **Our Lady of the Assumption** (1530), one of his most famous works (a work similar to this is housed in the church of the Frari di Venezia). It is enclosed by a magnificent frame, the work of Jacopo Sansovino. The Nichesola chapel contains the *Sepulchre of Bishop Nichesola*, also by Sansovino.

Cloister

The Chapter Cloister (it is considered to be the cloister of the cathedral) is a harmonious and highly evocative place. Built in the 12th century on the site where the original religious edifice of the Early Christian age stood - several ancient mosaics are still visible -, it is commonly known as the "most beautiful cloister in the city". Of particular

Photo above: Cathedral - detail of the portal with the beautiful porch designed by Master Nicolò
Photo below: Cathedral - remains of the original 9th century Cathedral.

interest and beauty is the side with a double order of arches surmounted by pairs of columels.

Chapter Library

This was the library which belonged to the "Chapter", that is to say to the congregation of the canons of the Cathedral.
It is a collection of extraordinary value in that it houses manuscripts, codices, miniatures, incunabula and very ancient documents. The foundation of the Library dates back to the 5th century and is therefore probably the first to be instituted in Italy

and one of the first at the international level. With regard to the wealth of material it contains and in view of its rarity, the library represents a fundamental source of information for scholars. Some of the documents of greatest value include: the *Codex of Justinian* (6th century), *De Civitate Dei* by Saint Augustine, *Institutions of Gaius* and an original codex of the 5th century. Several of the documents kept here are mentioned by the poet Petrarch who, in the course of his research, found Cicero's *Letters*. Annexed to the Library is the **Archive of the Canons**, rich in parchments and documents.

Canonical Museum

This is a small but interesting collection of paintings and sculptures. There are works which date to the 12th century: artists present include Francesco Morone, Francesco Torbido, Giovanni Falconetto, Liberale da Verona, Paolo Farinati and many others.

The Assumption of the Virgin - one of Titian's most famous works (1530). The splendid frame is the work of Sansovino.

Palazzo Miniscalchi - Miniscalchi Museum

The building was erected in the 15th century and modified and extended in the 19th. Of the primitive construction, the facade, frescoed and embellished with pointed windows, remains. A Museum has been set up inside: its rooms house 16th century and 18th century furnishings. There is a precious collection of sculptures, pottery and weapons of the Renaissance era, as well as an interesting collection of paintings and drawings.

Palazzo Forti - Gallery of Modern and Contemporary Art

It is housed in the eighteenth century **Palazzo Forti** (former Emilei, and at one time, the house of Ezzelino da Romano). One section is dedicated to the greatest artists of the nineteenth century and the early twentieth century; another sector, on the other hand, is reserved for contemporary art.

Church of Sant'Eufemia

This religious edifice, substantially modified in the 18th century, reveals the original Gothic architecture in its double lancet windows and in the portal of the facade. The interior has a single nave. Here the visitor can admire the fine *Dal Verme Chapel* (14th century), which maintains intact its Gothic features. It is embellished with paintings by Francesco Caroto, Brusasorci, (*Sarcophagus of the Dal Verme family*) and Martino da Verona.

Church of San Giovanni in Foro

Only the right-hand side (brick and stone) of this religious edifice is visible, extending along the Corso dei Borsari. The portal in pure Renaissance style is linear and elegant. Between its high windows is a work by Brusasorci depicting the *Deposition of Christ*. The interior has been substantially modified.

Porta Borsari

The remains of the Porta Borsari represent one of the most important examples of Roman civilization. Built in the 1st century A.D. along the boundary wall, it consists of two large fornices surmounted by gables. Pilasters rise up at the sides of the latter. This harmonious and solemn structure constituted a model for Renaissance architecture and for that of Verona in particular.
It was the main gate of ancient Verona: it was from here that the Via Postumia (link with the outside) and the great decuman road (the city's principal thoroughfare) departed.

Corso Cavour

This is the monumental, élegant and lively city thoroughfare which crosses part of the historic centre. It is flanked by splendid town houses for the most part dating back to the sixteenth and seventeenth century.
- **Giolfino's House**; this was the residence of the painter Giolfino. The facade bears traces of ancient frescoes;
- **Palazzo Carnesali** (16th century);
- **Palazzo Carlotti**, a monumental and solemn building built in the 17th century;

- **Palazzo Portalupi**, in neoclassical style;
- **Palazzo Muselli**, an original baroque building;
- **Palazzo Scannagatti-Gobetti**, in Renaissance architecture with elegant balconies and refined marble decorations.
- **Palazzo Bevilacqua**, an inestimable work by Sammicheli (1530): the lower floor is in ashlar-work - with a decentred main door -, and has large windows alternating with half-pillars; the upper floor, above a beautiful balustrade, has an alternating pattern of large and small windows separated by high fluted columns leaning on plinths.
- **Palazzo Canossa**, a beautiful building by Sammicheli partly modified in the 18th century. It is in the classical style: on the ground floor three deep portals succeed one another; on the upper floor the large windows are framed by high pilasters. Along the top part runs a splendid balustrade surmounted by statues dating back to the 18th century.
Within are paintings by Tiepolo (18th century), frescoes by Battista Moro and precious stuccoes. The building has housed important collections of paintings.
Along Corso Cavour stand the Churches of the Santi Apostoli and San Lorenzo.

Parish Church of the Santi Apostoli

It looks out onto the little square of the same name.
The remains which were brought to light in the area of the apse date the origin of the church back almost to the 8th century; it was subsequently reconstructed at the end of the 12th century and, after the damage suffered after the last world

war, it was almost entirely rebuilt. Of particular charm is the Romanesque bell tower.

Inside are frescoes of the 14th century and 16th century (Brusasorci, Lingozzi and Cignani).

The **Cloister** of the 12th century is a marvellous piece of architecture, and the small **Church of Saints Tosca and Teuteria** a remarkable example of Early Christian architecture of the 8th century, modified in subsequent eras when it acquired the role of chapel of the Bevilacqua family, whose funeral monuments can be admired.

Church of San Lorenzo

A beautiful church of Early Christian origin rebuilt in 1117 and subsequently extended. The facade, in terracotta and stone, is enclosed between two **towers** and adorned by an elegant porch.

The interior is unusual and atmospheric. It is divided into three naves by pilasters built of alternate fascias of terracotta and stone.

The upper fascia contains the matroneum, the place reserved for women. It is enriched by several frescoes by Brusasorci

Porta Borsari - built in the Roman age (1st century A.D.), it provided a model for Venetian Renaissance architecture.

(*Madonna among the Saints*, situated in the apse) and by Giolfino.

The Citadel

Its construction was commissioned by Gian Galeazzo Visconti with a view to providing better for the city centre.

Piazza Bra'

It is a vast area situated in the city centre and dominated by the imposing splendour of the Arena of Verona.

The Bra' - it is called thus by the Veronese as a shortening of the term "braida" which means "wide" - represents, together with the Piazza delle Erbe and the Piazza dei Signori, the heart of the city, a meeting place for the local people. It occupies the area where the Foro Boario once stood. It dates back to the 16th century: Sammicheli was largely responsible for the design of the urban layout and its completion through the construction of aristocratic residences.

It is embellished by a *garden*, the *Fountain of the Alps*, the *Equestrian Monument of Victor Emanuel II* (1883), and by aristocratic mansions such as *Palazzo Ottolini, Righettini, Guglienzi-Brognoligo* (by Sammicheli), *Campagna* and *degli Honorij*.

Worthy of note is the ***Palazzo della Gran Guardia*** which marks the boundary of the southern side of the square: it is a seventeenth century work designed by Domenico Curtoni in the style of Sammicheli. The building was completed in the 19th century and at that time acquired its neo-classical appearance. The ***Palazzo della Gran Guardia Nuova*** or ***Barbieri***, the Town Hall building, is a nineteenth century work of neo-classical inspiration. It supports the ***Main gates of the Brà***, huge sixteenth century arches with a crenellated coping built on the site of the ancient gate of the Brà. These create the monumental entrance to the square and were constructed at the behest of the Republic of Venice. They are flanked by a mighty fourteenth century **tower**, also crenellated.

Mention should also be made of the so-called **Listone**, a wide pavement (commonly known as the "marciapiedone") which runs alongside the town houses and serves as a meeting place for the Veronese. Near the Main Gates of the Bra' are the **Philharmonic Academy**, the **Philharmonic Theatre** (created by Francesco Bibiena, it was one of the most famous eighteenth century theatres) and the **Maffeiano Lapidary Museum**. The Museum, built in 1714 at the behest of Scipione Maffei, houses the collection of plaques, inscriptions, urns and vases, gathered together by Nichesola, as well as all the other finds which were subsequently acquired. These include Italic, Greek and Roman pieces originating from various archaeological areas in the Venetian region.

Left-hand photo: Piazza Bra' - panoramic view.
Opposite page:
photo above: Piazza Brà - this large square designed by the architect Sammicheli is dominated by the Verona Arena.
photo below: Piazza Bra' - the neo-classical Palazzo Barbieri (19th century), seat of the Municipality.

Maffeiano Lapidary Museum

Maffeiano Lapidary Museum - sarcophagus of the Roman age with a frieze depicting "The Muses".

Left-hand photo: Head of Jupiter.

Right-hand photo: Funerary stele of the Roman age.

Arena - Roman Amphitheatre

Impressive in terms of size and majestic in its architectural design, the Amphitheatre of Verona is second in size only to the Colosseum in Rome.

More commonly known as the Arena, it was built in the first half of the 1st century A.D.: it is in fact known that the construc-tion had already been complet-ed by 30 A.D.

It was located outside the walls dating back to the Republican age: from the 3rd century on-wards, at the behest of Gal-lienus, it was incorporated with-in the defensive walls for mo-tives of safety.

It has an elliptical plan which develops around the inner square measuring 73.68 x 44.43 metres. The external part on the other hand extends to a size of 138.77 x 109.52 metres (taking into consideration the outer-most ring, which has now col-lapsed, the axes measured 152 m. and 122 m.). The architectur-al structure of the Arena was composed of concentric rings.

On the outside are two orders of 72 arches separated by 73 pillars of brick and ashlars of

the pink stone of Verona measuring around two metres.

Originally it had two surrounds: only part now remains of the outer one owing to the devastation caused by the earthquakes of 1117 and 1183: this magnificent residue consisting of four arcades is known as the **wing**. It was more that 30 metres high. This sector was joined to the main inner architectural structure, which gives the Arena its present-day external appearance, by an ambulatory (4.40 metres) covered by a barrel vault. It was more than 18 metres high.

Other ambulatories link a third and then a fourth ring. The entire structure of the walls with ambulatories at intervals is made up of radial walls supporting the tiers of seats consisting of 44 steps. These have a concentric layout and follow the direction of the ellipsis of the amphitheatre.

At the centre is the arena, the inner platea, that is to say the space where gladiatorial games once took place.

An ingenious system of pipes, which ran under the floor of the ambulatories, allowed for the elimination of rainwater.

Various underground rooms were used as storehouses. The staircases leading to the various sectors of the tiers of seats departed from the ambulatories.

The cavea area of the Arena was almost completely rebuilt between 1569 and 1680. Nowadays it hosts magnificent operatic performances which find in this solemn and monumental venue, a particularly prestigious stage setting and an extremely atmospheric framework.

In the past, top-class theatrical events have been held here: among the many, worthy of special mention was the wonderful production of Romeo and Juliet in which Eleonora Duse gave an outstanding performance in the role of the female protagonist.

Today the Arena can boast 23,000/25,000 seats. In the Roman age it could seat up to 30,000 people.

The ancient amphitheatre, as was the case with other constructions, was used in ancient times to host performances which included gladiatorial combats, as well as the no less cruel and terrible *venationes*, that is to say the hunting of wild animals by these same gladiators. With the fall of the Roman empire and then with the ending of the *gladiatorial games*, the amphitheatre of Verona, used for a short time for institutional purposes such as the administration of justice and the execution of capital punishments, became an ideal venue for tournaments and jousts between knights.

In the photos: the Arena was the ancient Roman amphitheatre where gladiatorial combat took place as well as bloody battles between the latter and wild animals.

The performances

Gladiatorial games
These performances were held in the Amphitheatre in the Roman age: they consisted of battles between gladiators and the hunting of wild animals. The fighting took place in the Arena and drew an enormous crowd.

Tournaments and jousts
These performances were held in the Arena from the Middle Ages onwards. They consisted of competitions of skill or fights between knights.

Operatic events
The ancient Amphitheatre, now in operation once more after careful restoration, provides a venue for important cultural events including the famous Opera Season.

Wall of Gallienus

These are the ruins of the wall commissioned by the emperor Gallienus (end of the 3rd century A.D.), encompassing the Roman Amphitheatre within the city's defensive walls.

Church of San Nicolò dei Teatini

This building, of mediaeval origin, is of baroque architecture and was built in 1627 by L. Pellesina. The facade is the one belonging to the church of San Sebastiano. The extensive interior houses an admirable painting by Mattia Preti depicting *Saints Gaetano and Avellino* (2nd chapel on the left) and works by Orbetto, Bassetti, Balestra and numerous other local artists, who were among the most important of the seventeenth and eighteenth centuries.

Church of San Fermo Maggiore

This is an articulated architectural complex consisting of the superimposition of two churches.

The lower church, built in the mid-11th century, rose on the site where Saints Fermo and Rustico (361) were martyred and where, earlier on, popular devotion had resulted in the construction of a votive chapel (5th century) and later a small religious building (8th century). The upper church, begun approximately in the same period, was principally developed in the 14th century when the Benedictine monks who occupied the monastery were replaced by Franciscans (1261): the architectural complex then assumed its present-day form

and, in the perfect harmony between Romanesque and Gothic and in the admirable fusion of its pictorial and chromatic contents, provided one of the most important examples of Italian art.

Facade

Complex and monumental, it is of substantially Romanesque design. The lower fascia has a large central portal accentuated by a sequence of round ribbed arches and raised on a flight of steps. On the right-hand side the surface is divided by slender pilasters and by a hanging porch (*tomb of Giovanni da Tolentino*); on the left, enclosed in a hanging prothyrum, is the *sarcophagus of Aventino Fracastoro*.

A loggia runs above this lower sector of the facade.

The upper fascia of the facade has an alternating pattern of brick and stone. Four large and soaring single lancet windows open out at the centre.

The upper part is pictthed and surmounted by three Gothic cusps.

It is particularly interesting to take a walk around the outside of the church in order to appreciate the exceptional articulation of the apses.

Interior

Upper church

It corresponds to the churches of Franciscan type with a single nave and is spacious and extremely interesting owing to its measured spatiality and the works which decorate it.

The magnificent wooden keeled **ceiling** is painted with depictions of the *Saints*.

On the counterfacade, in the lunette, is a fine **Crucifixion** probably executed by Turone

(14th century); on the wall are fragmentary frescoes of the 14th and 15th centuries, including a *Last Judgement* by Martino da Verona.

Along the right-hand wall, among the numerous works, worthy of special mention are the *Martyrdom of Franciscan Saints* (painted in the 14th century); the *Nichesola Altar* of classical design (16th century); the **Choir of angels with a cartouche**: remains of the frescoes by Stefano da Verona; the **Pulpit** in wood and painted marble (Antonio da Mestre, 14th century). Mention should also be made of the Brenzoni Chapel which contains the *baptistery* and houses funeral monuments including the **Sepulchre of Barnaba da Morano**. A further mention should be made of the *Pietà*, an interesting sculpted group in high-relief of the 15th century.

The right-hand apse contains the beautiful Alighieri Chapel of Renaissance design: it contains *funeral monuments* by Sammicheli, early works. In addition there is a remarkable *Crucifixion* by Brusasorci.

The **Presbytery** is without doubt the essential nucleus of the church both owing to its striking architectural design as well as the pictorial works which decorate it.

In front of the Great Chapel is a circle of Ionic columns or *tornacoro* (1573).

Church of San Fermo Maggiore - a monumental complex consisting of an upper church and a lower one.

Church of San Fermo Maggiore - interior - The apse of the lower church.
Monument of Nicolò Brenzoni, fresco by Pisanello and sculpture by Nanni di Bartolo.

On the external part of the triumphal arch are the frescoes of the Giottesque school depicting *Daniele Gusmerio* and *Guglielmo Castelbarco* (14th century), the *Coronation of the Virgin* by Lorenzo Veneziano, *Stories of St. Francis* and *Stories of the Madonna*. Other paintings of the 14th century are housed in the interior and on the vault.

Next to the presbytery is the chapel of St. Antony where the visitor can admire the *altar piece of St. Antony and other Saints* by Liberale da Verona. In the adjacent chapel is the precious and richly ornamented *Monument of the Della Torre family* by A. Briosco. In the left-hand transept are the **Madonna and Saints** by Francesco Caroto (1538), the fine **Monument to Nicolò Brenzoni** executed by Nanni di Bartolo in the first half of the 15th century (it is surmounted by a curtain held open by two angels) and the magnificent **Annunciation** by Pisanello, a work of delicate and refined workmanship and one of the most important examples of Gothic: the painting is situated behind the funeral monument.

Lower church

The simplicity and severity of the Romanesque architecture is the first thing that strikes the visitor. The church has three naves divided by pillars. The central one is divided into two parts by pillars of smaller dimensions. The fine **capitals** show workmanship of an archaic type. The *frescoes* date back to the 11th-13th century.

Opposite page: the layout of the apses in the Church of San Fermo Maggiore.

Juliet's Tomb - Chapel of San Francesco al Corso

Juliet's tomb, a marble sarcophagus of the 13th-14th century, is situated in the former **Convent of the Franciscans**.

Inside the Convent mention should be made of the **Cloister** and the baroque *chapel of St. Francis*. This - also referred to in common usage as the "church" - houses remarkable paintings by Caroto, Brusasorci, Balestra and Campagna, by whom there is a fine *Annunciation*.

In several adjacent rooms a **Fresco Museum** has been set up: it contains detached frescoes of various epochs which originate from many buildings in Verona.

Church of the Holy Trinity

A precious example of Veronese Romanesque, it is a construction of the 11th-12th century.

The facade has accentuated slopes: it is embellished by a porch and by an atrium containing the *sarcophagus of Antonia da Sesso* (15th century). The interior has a single nave enhanced by apses. The high and mighty bell-tower is worthy of note: it has a square plan and a covering of bricks alternating with fascias of stone.

The Franciscan Convent and the sarcophagus which according to tradition is the Tomb of Juliet.

Gavi Arch

Built in the 1st century B.C. by the architect Vitruvius (the famous author of treatises on art) for the Gavi family, it was knocked down at the end of the 18th century to allow for the passage of Napoleonic troops. It was rebuilt in its original form in 1932 at Castelvecchio, that is in a different site from the previous one, which corresponded to the present-day Corso Cavour.

This honorary monument is made up of a single high fornix surmounted by a gable. At the sides rises a pair of robust and tall pilasters containing a niche. The internal vault is covered with a beautiful lacunar ceiling.

Castelvecchio
Castelvecchio Bridge or Scaligero Bridge

An impressive and spectacular architectural-military work in brick: it is made up of three large arches and pillars in the form of a quadrangular tower.

The entire structure has a crenellated coping, thus accentuating the image of a mighty defensive work. It was built in the second half of the 14th century. Bombed during the second world war it was entirely reconstructed with salvaged materials.

The panoramic view of the River Adige is most impressive.

Gavi Arch - an arch of Roman origin (1st century A.D.), reconstructed in the 20th century.

Castelvecchio - an imposing fortress built at the behest of Cangrande II Della Scala in 1534.

Ponte di Castelvecchio or Ponte Scaligeri - a majestic work with three great arches which links Castelvecchio to Verona across the River Adige.

Castelvecchio

The grandiose complex of Castelvecchio, an actual fortress, was commissioned by Cangrande II della Scala in 1534 and linked to the other bank of the Adige by means of the Castelvecchio bridge. Its strategic function - it was integrated into the perimeter of the city walls - remained virtually intact under the Visconti who linked it to the so-called Citadel by a covered passage intended to guarantee safety of passage from one part of the fortified building to the other. With the passing of time the castle acquired various functions: it was a barracks, arsenal and also a prison. Napoleon commissioned had a barracks built in its interior. Its rooms hosted the protagonists of the Republic of Salò as well as providing the venue for the trial of Galeazzo Ciano, minister of Foreign Affairs and son-in-law of Mussolini. After 1923 it underwent radical modification and restoration and was then used as the Municipal Museum. The same happened after the damage caused during the last world war: the restoration works of the post war led to the formation of the Municipal Picture Gallery.

Castelvecchio, built in the area of the ancient little church of San Martino, of which some remains are visible, has a complex structure and an irregular perimeter enhanced by seven towers, the largest of which is the Keep. It is surrounded by a moat divided into two sectors by a bridge: one part has two courtyards and a double boundary wall; the other, of rectangular shape, has a single courtyard and a single defensive wall. The restoration works brought to light parts of Castelvecchio which had been forgotten, such as the *Morbio Postern*, sectors of the primitive church of San Martino and a sector of the castle rampart.

Photo above: inner courtyard of Castelvecchio.
Opposite page: The equestrian statue of Cangrande I della Scala, a fourteenth century work executed for the sepulchral monument to the ruler of Verona.

Castelvecchio Municipal Museum

It houses one of the most interesting collections of Italian and European art. The museum, which since 1957, when the radical restoration of the fortress complex was carried out, has been organized along modern and functional lines, is spread over around thirty rooms and includes various sectors: sculpture, Italian and foreign painting, antique weapons and also the ancient city bells.

There is a vast display of **sculpture**, especially of pieces relating to the Veronese Romanesque. Among the most important works are:

- the **Crucifix**, a work in tuff by the so-called Master of the Crucifixes: it is a work of the 14th century and originates from the church of San Giacomo di Tomba;

- **sepulchre of Saints Sergius and Bacchus**: a precious sculpted work in bas-relief of 1179.

- sculptures of the 14th century including **Saint Cecilia and Saint Catherine**;

- **equestrian statue of Cangrande I della Scala**: it originates from the della Scala tombs near the church of Santa Maria Antica where it has been replaced with a copy. It is one of the most important works of fourteenth century art;

- *jewels of the Lombard epoch, Early mediaeval glass*;

The Castelvecchio Museum houses one of the most detailed and most important records of **painting** in the national field.

There is a remarkable collection of parts of frescoes and paintings of the fourteenth century.

The jewels in the collection of Gothic masters are the **Madonna of the Quail** attributed to Pisanello, and in the Madonna of the Rosegarden, attributed to Stefano da Verona: both interpret the international Gothic style

with the utmost refinement and harmony, as testified to by the extreme care paid to subtle details.

Painting of Venetian influence finds examples of intense lyricism in the **Crucifixion** by Jacopo Bellini (also represented here with a *Madonna of Humility*) and in the **Madonna and Child** by Gentile Bellini.

The work of Andrea Mantegna, a painter who had a strong influence on Veronese artists, is amply represented. Among the works displayed, worthy of particular mention is the **Holy Family**.

In addition, the museum houses works by Altichiero (*Boi Polyptych*), Domenico Morone, Marco Basaiti, Giovanni Mansueti, Vit-

Castelvecchio Municipal Museum - one of the rooms in the Museum. Opposite page: Crucifix, a fourteenth century work in tuff executed by the Master of the Crucifixes.

tore Carpaccio (*Saints Catherine and Veneranda*), Antonio Vivarini, Francesco Morone (fresco of the *Madonna enthroned among Saints*), Francesco dai Libri, Girolamo dai Libri (*Crib of the rabbits, Madonna of the oak, Madonna of the umbrella, Madonna Maffei*), Brusasorci, Farinati, Cavazzola, Liberale da Verona (*Madonna of the goldfinch, Adoration of the shepherds, Nativity with St. Jerome*), Carlo Crivelli (*Madonna of the Passion*), Lorenzo Lotto, Francesco Caroto (*Young boy with a puppet, Portrait of a monk*), Paolo Veronese (*Deposition*), Jacopo Tintoretto (*Concert*), G.B. Tiepolo, Luca Giordano, Francesco Guardi (*Landscape, Sketch for the ceiling of Ca' Rezzonico*) and Andrea Mantegna (*Christ carrying the cross, Holy Family*). Among the foreign artists whose works are exhibited are J. Daret, Van Cleef, G. Jordaens and Rubens.

Sepulchre of Saints Sergius and Bacchus
A splendid Romanesque work of the 12th century.

Relief of Saint Martin by an unknown sculptor
A high-relief in tuff depicting Saint Martin on horseback. The vertical trend of
the composition and the artist's vibrant, modular use of outline, places this
work within the Gothic tradition.

Statue of Saint John the Baptist

It is a fourteenth century work executed in tuff. The choice of material, the extremely concise features and the, at times, cursory, almost crude style make this a highly expressive work. The figure of the Baptist bears the evangelical symbol in his hand.

St. Jerome in the Desert

This work was executed by Jacopo Bellini, a 15th century Venetian artist. The panel was painted in 1436, at the time of his stay in Verona. It is characterised by a skilful use of colour in the Venetian tradition which, in this painting, is mainly expressed in monochrome shades.

Holy Family - Mantegna
Mantegna was active in Verona in the mid-15th century, bringing to the city his Renaissance background. With the Altar-piece of Saint Zeno (but also previously with the fresco depicting Saint James) he brought about a decisive shift in local art, which was still based on the Gothic tradition. Mantegna was later to inspire many local artists, Morone in particular. The Holy Family attributed to him is probably a late work.

Madonna of the Passion by Carlo Crivelli

This small panel takes its name from the depiction of the instruments of the Passion (lance, nails, ladder, column) in the left-hand part of the painting, which do not concern Christ but rather a group of men. A beautiful image of the Madonna stands out in the central part. The work combines both Gothic and Renaissance features.

Madonna of the Milk by Jacopo Tintoretto

This Venetian artist, among the most celebrated of the 16th century, is represented in the Museum by various works of art, including the Crib (or Adoration of the Shepherds) and the Concert of the Muses. The Madonna of the Milk is an expression of his mature period: the application of the colours and the warm effects of the light create a highly-balanced composition.

Madonna of the Rosary by Stefano da Verona
This is a late-Gothic work of refined workmanship. Attributed to Stefano di Verona - he was in fact of French origin - it comes from the Church of San Domenico. It depicts the Madonna and Child framed by exquisitely fashioned rose shoots amidst which bands of adoring Angels can also be glimpsed.

Nativity with Saint Jerome and Saint John the Baptist by Liberale da Verona
This work, similarly to others executed by this painter, reveals the attention which the Master paid to miniatures and to detailed decoration. His art shows the evident influence of the Gothic style.

Madonna of the Quail

It is generally attributed to Pisanello - though some critics maintain it is the work of Stefano da Verona - but is, however, ascribed to the former's early activity. The design of the composition and the importance of outline, which distinguishes all Gothic pictorial art, make it a work of exquisite and harmonious workmanship. The work originates from the Bernasconi Gallery.

Church of San Zeno in Oratorio

A Romanesque building built in the 13th century: it has a Gothic facade and contains statues and frescoes of the 14th and 15th century. Of novel interest is the stone which supports a funeral monument: tradition has it that it is the rock on which San Zeno used to sit and fish.

Church of Santa Teresa degli Scalzi

This octagonal plan church was built in the mid-17th century to a design by the architect Giuseppe Pozzo. Like many other Veronese buildings it was modified and largely rebuilt after the second world war. Inside, on the high altar, is a beautiful *Annunciation* by Antonio Balestra.

Porta Palio

The name recalls the feast of the Palio, the race which was run in this area during the Middle Ages. It is the work of Sammicheli and was built between 1542 and 1557.

The two facades differ from one another: one side - the inner one - has five robust fornices with pairs of pilasters at intervals. The surface is covered with ashlars creating an effect of solemnity and strength at one and the same time.

The external facade has three fornices flanked by pilasters, trabeated and adorned with statues.

Church of San Bernardino

This fifteenth century complex is dedicated to San Bernardino

of Siena who in 1422 came to the city to preach.

A large arcade precedes the religious edifice with its linear and soaring facade.

The central portal is refined by a marble arch which houses, around the circumference, the statues of various *Franciscan saints.*

The interior, like most Franciscan churches, has a single nave: in 1486, at the behest of local notables, a second smaller nave with chapels opening off it was added on the right-hand side.

The works which are housed here represent a remarkable example of Veronese painting in the first part of the sixteenth century.

The frescoes in the 1st chapel were painted by the artist Giolfino and represent *Stories of St. Francis.*

There are other paintings by Bonsignori, Morone and Caroto.

In the 5th chapel on the right (Avanzi chapel) is the magnificent *Crucifixion* by Francesco Morone, one of his finest works.

Inside is the polyptych of the *Passion* by Morando.

The masterpiece of the church is the **Pellegrini Chapel** designed by Michele Sammicheli and begun in the early 16th century: it represents one of the best examples of Veronese Renaissance architecture.

The room is skilfully balanced in spatial terms: it has a central plan enhanced by niches of varying sizes arranged on two orders.

The architectural development of the walls is completed by the lacunar ceiling. Various frescoes decorate the chapel.

Another room of noteworthy

interest is the **Morone Room** - it was the old Library - whose walls were entirely frescoed by Domenico and Francesco Morone.

The collection of paintings dates back to 1503; the subjects are the *Franciscan saints*, and on the wall opposite *Saints Francis and Clare, the Madonna and Child and the Sagramos Family*, who commissioned the work.

The basilica of San Zeno Maggiore, a splendid example of Romanesque art.

Basilica of San Zeno Maggiore

This is one of the masterpieces of Italian Romanesque art.

The primitive construction rose on the tomb of St. Zeno, one of the first bishops of Verona, and dates back to the 5th century. In the 9th century a new temple was erected, which was in its turn enlarged and covered by the basilica erected between 1120 and 1138 after an earthquake had largely devastated the original building. The subsequent modifications and enlargements are due to the work of Lombard masters. In the 14th century a polygonal apse was added: it was designed by Giovanni and Niccolò da Ferrara. At the beginning of the 19th century it was closed for worship and left in a state of abandonment. As a consequence of the discovery of the relics of the first Veronese bishops buried here and several pictorial and sculptural finds, the building underwent significant restoration works (the last dates back to 1988), which have restored it to its original splendour. The church is flanked by a lofty bell-tower dating back to the 11th century. On the opposite side is the **Tower** which was part of the thirteenth century Benedictine complex.

Facade

Harmonious and elegant, it reveals the division of the interior into three naves as a result of the varying height of the lateral and central parts and the slender pilasters which vertically accentuate it. A fine *rose window* - it is called *"the wheel of fortune"* owing to the sculptures depicting life's happy moments - embellishes the upper fascia underneath the gable. Horizontally, the facade is dotted with small double lancet windows.

There is a magnificent **portal** (thirteenth century work by Niccolò and assistants) within a *porch* resting on two lions and decorated with bas-reliefs depicting the *Evangelists* and *St. Zeno*. In the lunette is the effigy of *St. Zeno among cavalrymen and foot soldiers giving his blessing*.

The feature of greatest interest is a set of **48 bronze tiles**: they are a masterpiece of the art of the period. These, in extremely concise language and with great expressive impact, narrate *Episodes of the Old and New Testament* and *Miraculous episodes of the life of St. Zeno*.

To the side of the entrance is a very important bas-relief with episodes from the Old and New Testaments, and Theodoric astride the deer which is carrying him to Hades.

Right-hand photo: detail of the bas-reliefs on the portal.
Opposite page
photo above: the lunette of the main portal showing the effigy of Saint Zeno among cavalrymen and foot soldiers giving his blessing.
Photo below: the facade of the church is flanked by a tower which is part of the Benedictine convent.

Details of the bas-reliefs on the portal depicting the Evangelists and San Zeno.
Opposite page: the spacious and soaring interior of the Basilica of San Zeno.

Interior

Solemn, grandiose and, at the same time, very simple and linear, the complex articulation of the structure of the interior and its spatiality are breathtaking: the central nave is preceded by a staircase; the side naves are divided by pillars alternating with monolithic columns; at the far end is the presbytery - raised above the crypt - characterised by the soaring Gothic ribwork of the apse.

Of great effect is the fine **wooden lacunar ceiling**, a precious work of 1386.

Just inside the church is the **baptismal font**, octagonal in shape and sculpted in the 12th century from a single block of marble (work of Brioloto). The beautiful **Crucifix** is a 14th century work by Lorenzo Veneziano. The red porphyry **bowl** is a find of Roman origin probably originating from a thermal building.

A great many works of art embellish the interior. These include the cycle of **frescoes** of the 13th and 14th century (right-hand nave and pillars), in which scholars have identified at least two artists, identified by the names of "First Master of San Zeno" and "Second Master of San Zeno", without doubt fundamental to an understanding of the Veronese painting school of that period. Of further interest are *Saint Christopher* (known also as *King Pepin*), the *Madonna and Child*, the *Crucifixion* and *Saint Stephen*.

There are several interesting **altars**: the 1st on the right is Renaissance; the 2nd consists of material salvaged from a Romanesque structure; the altar in the left-hand nave (altar of Our Lady of Sorrows) is a baroque work.

The Basilica is brought to an admirable conclusion by the **presbytery**: it is raised above the crypt and. is completed by the soaring Gothic apse.

It is enclosed by a wooden surround and an **iconostasis** surmounted by statues depicting *Christ and the 12 Apostles*, a thirteenth century work by a Veronese artist. At the back is a wooden **choir** dating to the mid-15th century. Of further interest are the frescoes on the walls, including the *Annunciation* by Martino da Verona (it is on the entrance archway and has been repainted) and the *Abbot Capelli and his brothers* by R. Arvari. The frescoes in the apse are also by Martino da Verona. The *Crucifixion* situated above the door of the Sacristy is by the school of Altichiero. A fine *Annunciation* by the Master of Sant'Anastasia decorates the altar.

Among the sculptures a particular mention should go to the statue of St. Zeno (**"St. Zeno laughing"**), executed in the 14th century and the object of Veronese devotion. In polychrome marble, it shows the face of the black patron saint, who came originally from Africa. The basilica's most precious jewel is without doubt the magnificent **altar piece** by Andrea Mantegna. It is a triptych depicting the *Madonna and Child among the Angels and Saints* set in a gilded frame. On the altar step - the original is housed in the Louvre - *Episodes of the life of Christ* are represented. This painting, skilfully balanced in design and in perfect harmony with the tripartition caused by the structure of the frame, is a splendid example of Renaissance art.

Crypt

Seven great arches leaning on marble columns open onto this room, which was built in the 13th century. The friezes which adorn the capitals and the arched lintels are the work of Adamino da san Giorgio (1225). The ribbed vault is frescoed.

It houses the **urn** (a 12th century work) containing the relics of St. Zeno, which were found as a consequence of the research carried out in 1838. It is flanked by the *urns* of Saints Lucillo, Lupicino and Crescentiano.

Cloister

The Cloister - once annexed to the Convent of the church - can be reached from the left-hand

nave. It is an open space of harmonious and airy design and was built in the 12th century in the simple and elegant Romanesque style. It consists of a low arcade formed of double columns supporting round and Gothic arches and a canopy. On the northern side is an aedicule. Along the perimeter of the arcade are various sepulchral monuments, including that of the abbot of St. Zeno mentioned by Dante in his Purgatory and remains of frescoes mostly dating back to the 13th century, including one of the Giottesque school (*Madonna and Child with Saints Zeno and Benedict*). Of interest is the *Oratory* known as the *Oratory of St. Benedict*, constructed using materials of the Roman age.

The presbytery is raised above the crypt and terminates in an elegant Gothic apse.
Photo on previous page: The Cloister of the basilica of San Zeno Maggiore - it dates back to the 12th century and was part of the Benedictine convent.

Church of San Procolo

The 12th century church, substantially modified in the 16th century, was built on the remains of the Early Christian basilica erected around the 5th century A.D. It is only in recent years that careful restoration has saved the church which had fallen into ruins. The facade is extremely simple: it is embellished by a porch and two double lancet windows. The interior houses several interesting works including some paintings and two sarcophagi containing the relics of the first Christian bishops of the city. There is a fine **crypt** datable to around the 9th century: it has three naves, cross-vaults, and columns salvaged from an older building. On the walls are the remains of frescoes of the 12th century.

Veronetta

Veronetta is the name given to the part of the city which spreads out along the left bank of the River Adige: it was designated by this name in the early 19th century when a part of Verona passed under the Lombard-Veneto realm dependent on Austria and another remained under France.

Church of San Giorgio in Braida

This religious edifice was erected on the site of a small pre-existing church dedicated to the Saint and dating back to the 8th century on which, in the 11th century, a Benedictine convent was built. Its structure represents one of the most important examples of Veronese Renaissance architecture. Begun in the

Church of San Giorgio in Braida and the Adige embankment.

15th century - attributed to Antonio Rizzo and Sammicheli - it was later transformed in the 17th. The illustrious architect was responsible for the tiburium and the dome and, above all, the design of the interior, which is extremely harmonious and balanced in all its parts.

The facade is adorned with niches containing statues and with an elegant Serlian window. It was built in the 17th century.

The church houses a remarkable artistic heritage. Worthy of particular mention is the masterpiece by Paolo Veronese depicting **The martyrdom of St. George** (high altar in the apse) and the one attributed to Jacopo Tintoretto taking as its subject **The baptism of Christ**. There are fine works by Girolamo dai Libri **The Madonna and Child and Saints** (4th chapel on the left) and Moretto **Saint Cecilia among the Saints**. The depiction of the *Pentecost* is by Domenico Tintoretto; works by Brusasorci include a *Madonna among the Angels* (a work of great merit), *The fall of manna from Heaven* and the *Exorcism of the possessed man*; the latter is integrated into the *Triptych* by Francesco Caroto located in the 3rd chapel. At the sides of the Chancel is an admirable work by Girolamo Romanino taking

as its subject *Saint George presenting himself for judgment.* There is a charming **Cloister** annexed to the church, which was part of the ancient monastery.

Church of Santo Stefano

A Christian edifice already stood on this site in the 5th century; it was modified and enlarged in several stages and in the 12th century particularly, after it had been destroyed by the earthquake of 1117. The facade, in-between high buttresses, has a tuff and terracotta covering.

The remarkable interior has preserved to a large extent its mediaeval design and archaic atmosphere. The presbytery area is raised. The walls and chapels are decorated with frescoes of the 14th and 16th century. The statue of *St. Peter on the papal Chair* (right-hand nave) is of the fourteenth century.

Of particular interest is the apse whose 10th century architectural structure consists of an ambulatory (arcade with a circular trend) and columns and capitals from the original Early Christian building. Mention should be made of the baroque **Chapel of the Innocents**, so called because, according to tradition,

several of the "innocent children" whom Herod ordered to be slain are buried there, together with various martyrs. On the walls are paintings by Bassetto (*Veronese bishops*) and Orbetto (*The torture of the forty Veronese martyrs*). Immersed in the semi-darkness, the crypt is highly atmospheric: precious capitals surmount the columns, these too dating back to the Early Middle Ages. This apse too has an ambulatory.

Castel San Pietro

This fortress, built by the Visconti, was demolished and replaced in the 19th century owing to its strategic position. There is a magnificent panoramic view from the fortress.

Photo above: The Adige embankment and a glimpse of the Church of San Giorgio in Braida.
Photo below: The Adige embankment and Castel San Pietro.

Archaeological Area
Roman Theatre

This Theatre was built under Emperor Augustus and subsequently enlarged and embellished.

The building which can be seen nowadays is probably on a smaller scale than the original one. Located in an archaeological area of great interest, the construction was brought to light in the 18th century by Abbot Fontana: works proceeded throughout the 19th and 20th century thanks to Monga, Ghirardini and Avena.

Thanks to the salvaging of the structure and its restoration, the theatre is now back in full working order: nowadays it is the venue for seasons of performances of a high cultural level. Near the cavea are three terraces, one of which is largely occupied by the Convent of St. Jerome. The level part behind ends in the Castel san Pietro area.

Near the cavea of the theatre is the **Church of Saints Siro and Libera** originating from the 10th century and modified in the 16th and 17th century. There is an original facade with a hanging porch and a baroque staircase with a double flight of steps.

It contains several paintings (*Madonna and Saint Gaetano, Madonna and Saints Siro and Libera*), a fine eighteenth century *altar* (high altar) with marble inserts, a wooden *Choir* executed by Kraft in the 18th century and an *Annunciation* by Ridolfi.

A glimpse of the Roman Theatre and the tiny Church of Saints Siro and Libera.

Archaeological Museum

Above the Roman structure stands the Convent of St. Jerome in which the Archaeological Museum has been set up.

It houses an exhibition of archaeological materials of Roman Verona, which has been organized along modern and functional lines.

There is a rich and interesting collection of ceramics, mosaics, vases, sarcophagi and altars as well as many architectural fragments. There is a wealth of small bronzes, both Italic and Greek. Among the pieces of greatest importance are a *head* of the 1st century A.D. and the *Portrait of Pestrino* (1st century A.D.)

Archaeological Museum - a room in the Archaeological Museum and various mosaics (1st century A.D.) depicting Battle scenes between gladiators.

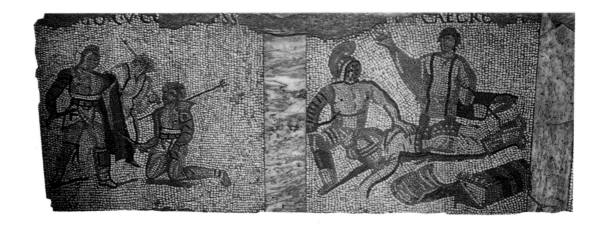

Archaeological Museum - mosaics of the Roman age dating back to the 1st century A.D..

Church of San Giovanni in Valle

This fine Romanesque construction was rebuilt in 1117 on the site where an older temple stood. The apsidal part is particularly beautiful - that on the right is the older part - with its elegant decoration of small hanging arches and a frieze depicting *Hunting scenes*. On the facade adorned with a porch is a fresco by Stefano da Verona depicting the *Madonna among the Saints*. At the side stands part of the ancient cloister with round arches leaning on small double columns: several tomb slabs lie along the arcade. The interior, which is of remarkable interest, has three naves and a raised presbytery.

It contains some admirable fourteenth century frescoes. Of great atmospheric impact is the **crypt** which houses the ***Sepulchre of Saints Simon and Jude*** dating back to the 4th century with precious bas-reliefs and another Sarcophagus, also of the 4th century, with the effigy of *a married couple* and *Saints Peter and Paul*.

Church of Santa Maria in Organo

The church looks out onto the square of the same name. Its solemn facade was executed by Sammicheli and added to the older one of Romanesque style. This religious edifice was in fact an ancient Benedictine convent erected in the 8th century and rebuilt in the 12th. Its final transformation took place at the end of the 15th century. The facade by Sammicheli is of marble and has three large deep portals - with pronounced half-columns at intervals - which occupy the entire height of the church. The soaring and elegant bell-tower was probably designed by the monk fra' Giovanni da Verona and built in the first half of the 16th century. The interior, harmonious and monumental in its Renaissance design, has three naves and four bays at the end of which, past a staircase, is the presbytery raised over the crypt.

Counterfacade:
- *Madonna in glory* (1533) by Savoldo

Central nave:
- frescoes by Francesco and Giovanni Caroto (right-hand wall) and Giolfino (left-hand wall) taking as their subject *Stories of the Old Testament* and, in the medallions, images of *Saints*. Along the right and left-hand naves are works by Pittoni, Farinati and, in the third chapel on the left, the magnificent work by Francesco Morone depicting the **Madonna with Saints Augustine and Zeno**.

The Presbytery is the most interesting part of the church. Among the works worthy of note are:
- the **Choir** in wooden marquetry, a marvellous work by fra' Giovanni da Verona: it consists of two orders of carved and inlaid stalls.

Photo above: the Romanesque Church of San Giovanni in Valle with what remains of the ancient cloister.
Photo below: the linear facade of the Church of San Giovanni in Valle.

The subjects depicted in the panels relate to *panoramic views, still lives* and the *Crucifixion*.

- a **candelabrum** and a **lectern** (by fra' Giovanni da Verona);
- *Santa Francesca Romana*, a beautiful altar piece executed by Guercino in 1639 (chapel in the far wall);
- *The Blessed Bernardo Tolomei*, painted by Luca Giordano;
- *"The Little Mule"*: this is the name given to this thirteenth century sculpture in painted wood depicting *Jesus entering Jerusalem on a she-mule*;
- paintings by Francesco Caroto, Paolo Farinati, Domenico Brusasorci, and Antonio Balestra. In the Sacristy, frescoed by Francesco and Domenico Morone with *Portraits of Olivetan monks*, are the splendid **chairbacks** in carved and inlaid wood, also by fra' Giovanni da Verona, and works by Brusasorci, who executed the paintings on the cupboards. The painting of *St. Francis and Saint Antony* is by Orbetto.

Crypt

The entrance to the crypt is situated in the presbytery, the original one having been closed in the 17th century owing to the construction of the staircase which led to the presbytery. The room is of pre-Roman design, which makes it one of the most important examples of Veronese architecture of the period. It has three naves whose columns with **capitals** are a residue of the original construction of the 8th century. On the altar is a precious marble *Madonna and Saints* of the 14th century.

Church of Santa Maria in Organo - the facade (work of Sammicheli) and the interior.

Church of San Tomaso Cantuariense

This church, dedicated to Saint Thomas archbishop of Canterbury, was built in the 15th century. The facade has fine Gothic windows. The interior has a single nave with a trussed roof. It contains the *tomb* of the architect Sammicheli who worked so prolifically in Verona (Zannoni, 1884). There is a fine painting by Girolamo dai Libri depicting *Saints Roch, Sebastian and Onofrio* (right-hand wall), as well as works by Farinati and Brusasorci. Mention should be made of the precious *organ* of baroque workmanship which, according to tradition, was used by Mozart when he was still very young.

Giusti Garden

Laid out in 1580, this delightful spot with its harmoniously designed flowerbeds is considered to be one of the most beautiful gardens in the country. It has a square plan subdivided into two parts: the lower one takes the form of a typical Italian garden in which, amidst the verdant hedges and the brilliant colours of the flowers, statues and fountains alternate. The upper part, on the other hand, is characterized by rows of cypresses and other trees. The garden also has a *maze* whose paths are lined by box hedges (created by Luigi Trezza in the 18th century). The architecture of the **Palazzo del Giardino Giusti**, rebuilt at the end of the 16th century, is in the classical style.

The Giusti Garden, a typical Italian garden with age-old trees and flowerbeds adorned with statues.

Church of Saints Nazaro and Celso

Before the church itself there is an imposing portico, flanked by two great columns supporting a tympanum.

Various works of art can be admired inside: among the most important are the statue of the *Madonna and Child* by the Master of Sant'Anastasia, the pictorial cycle taking as its subject *Saints Nazaro and Celso and other Saints* (Bartolomeo Montagna), and paintings by Bonsignori, Balestra and Farinati.

Most worthy of note is the **Chapel of Saint Blaise** (left-hand transept), a masterpiece by Beltramo di Valsolda (Lombard): the room has a square plan and is completed by a dome. On the altar is the *tomb of Saint Blaise and Saint Juliana*. The frescoes on the walls are by Bartolomeo Montagna, while in the dome they are by Giovanni Maria Falconetto and Girolamo Mocetto.

Near the church stands the **Votive chapel of Saints Nazaro and Celso**, whose frescoes are housed in the Fresco Museum.

Church of Santa Maria in Paradiso

Built in the 16th century it was substantially modified in the 19th. Inside are works by Balestra, Farinata and Liberale da Verona, as well as a *Crucifix* of the 14th century.

Opposite page: a splendid view of the Giusti Garden.

Palazzo Pompei - Natural Science Museum

This building, designed by Sammicheli in the mid-16th century, has a solemn and monumental appearance: wide arched windows on the ground floor and an airy open gallery on the upper floor. It houses the Natural Science Museum - the archaeological collection also used to be exhibited here - which contains a vast record of prehistoric flora and fauna as well as a remarkable collection of minerals and fossils. The exhibition is spread over 19 rooms on two floors. The materials are exhibited in glass showcases and suitably catalogued according to type and region of origin.

The Palazzo Pompei was built by the architect Sammicheli in the mid-16th century.

The Adige Embankment

The river winds its way through the city forming large loops. It is crossed by numerous bridges which link the historic centre with the part of the city known as "Veronetta". Apart from the Roman Ponte Pietra and the Ponte di Castelvecchio, the other bridges were built in the 19th century (Ponte della Ferrovia) or in the 20th. Among those worthy of mention are the Ponte del Risorgimento designed by Pier Luigi Nervi and the Ponte della Vittoria built by Fagiuoli in the period immediately after the war.

In addition, the Adige Embankment offers spectacular views over the city and its monuments. Particularly atmospheric are those which sweep over to Castelvecchio from the *Lungadige Cangrande*. The area known as *Regaste San Zeno* and the *Lungadige San Giorgio* are especially beautiful; the latter stretches past the church of San Giorgio in Braida and borders on the defensive walls of the Austrian epoch.

A circuit of the walls Walls and ramparts

When Verona became a Roman colony a circuit of walls was built with two gates in it: of these two only the Porta dei Leoni now remains. Two bridges were constructed over the Adige, the Ponte di Pietra and the Ponte Postumio.

The system of fortifications of the della Scala era and of the Venetian period marked the limits of the city's enlargement and constituted the fortified perimeter which also includes the castles of San Felice and San Pietro and numerous ramparts.

The city gates, with the exception of the Porta dei Leoni and the Porta Borsari, were built in the 16th century when the city was fortified. The work was entrusted to the architect Sammicheli.

In the northern part of the city is the **Porta San Giorgio** (16th century) followed by the *rampart of San Giorgio*. A little further on the remains of the *Castello di san Pietro* are visible. Next is the *Castello san Felice* and, after a long stretch of fortifications we reach the **Porta San Zeno** which has a terracotta and stone facade with three apertures and is decorated with coats-of-arms.

Then comes the **Porta Vescovo** with three fornices and a higher central part. It is made of brick with stone decorations and was renovated under the Austrians. After the *rampart of the Maddalene* and *the rampart of Campo Marzo* comes the **Porta della Vittoria Nuova** (19th century), then the *rampart of the Trinity* and the **Porta Nuova**. This provides access to Piazza Bra'. Built in the 16th century by Sammicheli, it was enlarged in the 19th century with the addition of the two lateral wings. The *Rampart of S. Spirito* follows and after that the **Porta del Palio**, the *Rampart of San Bernardino*, the *Rampart of San Zeno*, the *Rampart of San Procolo* and the *Rampart of Spain* (Sammicheli, mid-16th century). Next is the **Porta Fura** or **Porta Catena**, distinguished by three fornices of various epochs.

Excursions in the immediate environs

The environs of Verona encompass the resorts scattered over the amphitheatre of the lovely hills around and those of the so-called "Campagna".

Many of the villages in the vicinity, once independent, are

Panoramic view of the Adige embankment and Ponte Pietra.

now perfectly integrated into the outlying area of the city which, after its huge urban expansion, reached as far as these ancient centres and beyond. Others, especially those on the slopes of the Lessini mountains and those scattered along the road which leads to nearby Lake Garda (all in the space of a few kilometres), make for a pleasant excursion.

The walks on offer in the immediate environs provide an opportunity to discover hidden corners of great beauty and to enjoy the magnificent panoramic views, such as those which can be had from the **Strada dei Colli** or from the square of **Castel san Pietro** or the **square of the Colle di San Leonardo**. Beyond Porta Vescovo lies **San Michele Extra**, a small centre

Porta San Zeno - with three fornices and a terracotta and stone facade.

which has sprung up around a Convent.

In the vicinity stands the **Sanctuary of the Madonna di Campagna**. This religious edifice was built to commemorate the peace treaty of Cateau-Cambresis (1559) which marked the peace between France and Spain. For this reason the sanctuary still bears the name of Santa Maria della Pace.

It was designed by the architect Sammicheli, but subsequent in-

Sanctuary of Our Lady of Lourdes

The Sanctuary was built at St. Leonard's fort on the hill of the same name along the city's boundary wall. The works to build the sanctuary began on the 11th February 1908 on the occasion of the 50th anniversary of the apparitions of Our Lady of Lourdes. Its consecration took place in March 1909: the solemn ceremony was officiated by the Bishop of Lourdes Mons. Schöepfer. The religious edifice, in the course of the second world war, suffered severe bomb damage (1945) and only the statue of the Madonna survived, executed in 1908

by the sculptor Ugo Zannoni, which was then housed in the Church of the Stigmata whilst a new church was built.

On the occasion of the centenary of the apparitions of Our Lady in Lourdes, Cardinal Urbani decided to give the miraculous statue of

the Immaculate Conception a seat worthy of its importance: the renovation works of the sanctuary began in 1958 and continued until 1968: the latter, designed by the architect Paolo Rossi, was erected at the sanctuary of St. Leonard's fort which, built by the Austrians at the beginning of the 19th century, had subsequently been used as a political prison during the second world war. The church was embellished with works by V. di Colbertaldo and A. Del Vecchio.

The sanctuary is the destination of religious pilgrimages from the city and from its environs.

In the photos: panoramic views of Lake Garda, one of the Veronese people's favourite destinations.

terventions have partly modified the structure. The outside of the sanctuary is characterized by an arcade with Tuscan columns.

Various interesting works of art are housed inside. Worthy of special mention is the *Deposition* by Felice Brusasorci (1st altar on the right), the *Nativity of Jesus* by Farinati (2nd altar on the right); a *Madonna assumed into Heaven* by Ridolfi (1st altar on the left) and the *Flagellation* by Brusasorci (2nd altar on the left). Set into the fine architectural structure of the *great altar* is a fourteenth century fresco depicting a *Madonna and Child among the Saints*.

Another itinerary of great interest is the one starting out from Porta San Giorgio.

In **Avesa** a visit may be made to the *Parish* and *Church of Santa Maria della Camaldola*, which has a Romanesque structure embellished with a Renaissance portal and, inside, frescoes of the 14th and 15th century.

In **Quinzano**, in the *Parish church*, is a beautiful fresco by Antonio Badile (*Madonna among the Saints and Angels*). In the *Church of San Rocco* the visitor can appreciate the original architectural solutions exhibited by the chapels in the presbytery.

In **Parona di Valpolicella** the beautiful *Villa Erbisti* (19th century) is well worth a visit, as is the small *church of San Dionigi*, whose fourteenth century structure was erected above a building of the 9th century. The interior houses fourteenth century frescoes.

Walks around Lake Garda, Monte Baldo and the Lessinia

Lake Garda, the largest of the Italian lakes, is barely 30 km. from Verona and thus constitutes a natural appendix to the city. The lovely lakeside villages are popular tourist destinations, not least because of the efficient

The Verona Fair

Established at the end of the 19th century to serve as a market, in 1930 it was converted into an independent Body which organizes a series of exhibitions relating to agriculture, zootechnics, farm machinery and typical products.

In addition, the fair puts on special exhibitions for the display of specific products and activities in some way linked with the fields of agroindustry and health, such as thermal therapy, mushroom growing, wine growing and the preparation of medicinal herbs.

In conjunction with these exhibitions is the one held relating to marble and its by products.

The Museum of Italian Carriages has been set up in the pavilions of the Verona Fair.

and functional accommodation facilities they provide. Of particular interest are the towns which overlook the Veronese shore: the fortified city of **Peschiera** (together with Verona, Legnago and Mantova it was part of the Hapsburg "quadrilateral") and the town of **Lazise** (ancient outpost first of the Della Scala family and later of Venice, with remains of the mediaeval epoch). A little further north is **Bardolino**, a centre in the area which produces the famous D.O.C. wine. Next comes **Garda**, a resort which gave its name to the lake: overlooking the splendid inlet enclosed by the **San Vigilio** point, it is one of the most atmospheric and famous spots on the lake. **Monte Baldo** is an area of great environmental interest. The itinerary runs along part of the course of the Adige and then starts to climb the mountain slopes which reach a height of above 2000 metres. The walk is extremely varied and rich in vegetation with breathtaking scenic views of the plain below and Lake Garda.

Hiking paths have been established over the mountainside and sports facilities and ski runs built on top.

The **Lessinia** is a habitat of great environmental significance and, owing to its specific characteristics, it provides a unified setting in terms of both scenery and morphology, as well as culture and history.

This region lies between the Po plain and the foothills of the Alps and is occupied by a hill and mountain system known as Monti Lessini which ranges between 800 and 1200 metres.

The entire area is scattered with delightful sleepy villages and solitary shepherd's huts. The woodland of the piedmont strip gives way to extensive pastures on the higher ground and open, solitary expanses.

Enchanting panoramic views sweep across the plain and the mountains further off. There are a number of places of special geological interest: caves, Karstification.

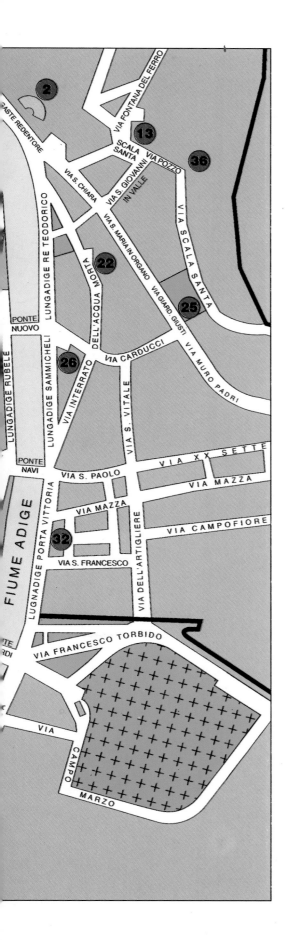

Main Monuments and Museums

Roman Verona
1. Piazza delle Erbe
2. Roman Theatre
3. The Arena amphitheatre
4. Gavi Arch
5. Porta Borsari
6. Porta Leona
7. Ponte Pietra

Communal Verona
8. Piazza dei Signori: Palazzo del Comune and the Old Market Courtyard (Della Ragione Staircase)
9. Basilica of San Zeno
10. San Lorenzo
11. The Cathedral
12. San Stefano
13. San Giovanni in Valle
14. SS. Trinità
15. SS. Apostoli

Della Scala Verona
8. Piazza dei Signori: Della Scala Residences and Tombs.
16. Castelvecchio
17. San Fermo
18. Sant'Anastasia
19. Sant'Eufemia
20. Juliet's House
21. Juliet's Tomb

Venetian Verona
8. Piazza dei Signori: Loggia del Consiglio
22. Santa Maria in Organo
23. San Giorgio in Braida
1. Piazza Erbe: Palazzo Maffei
25. Giusti Garden
26. San Tomaso Cantuariense
27. San Nazaro
28. San Bernardino, Pellegrini Chapel, Morone Room
29. San Nicolò
30. Porta Palio
31. Porta Nuova

Museums
16. Castelvecchio Museum
32. Municipal Museum of Natural History
33. Gallery of Modern Art
34. Miniscalchi Erizzo Foundation Museum
35. Maffeiano Lapidary Museum
36. African Museum

Map by kind permission of Azienda di Promozione Turistica di Verona.